Parental Burnout:

How to cope with the stress and exhaustion of parenting.

Danielle J. Carlson

TABLE OF CONTENT

INTRODUCTION

Please have a seat, wonderful parents, and let's chat. When parenting seems like a crazy roller coaster, this book is like your best buddy. Do you ever have days where you're trying to balance a million things and you wonder if other people understand? Yes, we do.

Simple narratives of worn-out parents just like you are all that are needed, no fancy language. I'll be sharing tips and tricks for managing the challenging aspects of parenting without turning it all into a research project. We're all in this together, figuring it out one dirty day at a time, so let's get down to the specifics of stress and tiredness.
Are you prepared to go on this adventure?

Have you ever experienced what Sarah, our colleague, is going through?

Sarah was on the verge of parental burnout as the days merged into an unrelenting schedule of changing diapers, restless nights, and unceasing demands. The once-bright joy of motherhood has gradually given way to an unwavering, chronic tiredness.

With two children to raise and a busy career to balance, Sarah felt like she had the entire world on her shoulders. Her head was filled with the incessant sound of sobbing, and every night felt like it went on forever. She tried everything to shake off the remorse and inadequacy that were creeping into her mind.

The breaking point came one frantic morning when she was trying to balance a tight work deadline with getting the kids ready for daycare. She was dancing frantically when she felt a wave of extreme exhaustion sweep over her. Tears filled her eyes, and she felt incredibly empty. In the middle of the confusion, Sarah recognized she was drowning in parental burnout rather than merely tiredness at that same time.

The cost went beyond her personal emotional terrain. She had hardly had dinner talks with her husband these days, only the routine trade of logistics and child-rearing responsibilities. There was a hint of strain in the previously pleasant family trips. Their parenting experience appeared to be marked by a flickering spark that was on the verge of going out.

Sarah and her partner made the decision to reevaluate their objectives after realizing the necessity. They implemented a more sustainable regimen that allowed for times of self-care, and they sought out assistance from friends and family. By keeping lines of communication open and assigning each other tasks, they were able to gradually remove the exhaustion that had enveloped their home.

Parental burnout, you see, is a condition in which parents feel exhausted and overburdened from caring for their children; they feel as though they are at their breaking point and require time away.

Imagine parents who feel both physically and emotionally worn out from caring for their children, as if they have expended all of their energy in doing so. The demands of one's parents can be likened to running on empty batteries.

Experiencing parental burnout is akin to attempting to balance a hard career and a second job at the same time. It's the sensation of being overextended, where parents become exhausted and stressed out due to the mounting obligations from both job and parenthood.

The effects of parental burnout can be seen in our household. We can become worn out, anxious, and less able to handle things as a result. This could have an impact on how we connect with each other and our kids, which could strain our family bonds.

Parents that go through burnout exhaust themselves emotionally and physically. This weariness could make them less patient and receptive to their kids' demands. Parental communication may be hampered by stress, which may result in miscommunication or confrontations. In general, parental burnout can lead to a difficult environment in the family that lowers the caliber of interactions and relationships.

CHAPTER 1

RECOGNIZING THE SIGNS OF PARENTAL BURNOUT

Being a parent is a fulfilling but difficult journey that requires a large time, energy, and emotional commitment. The pressures of contemporary life can occasionally cause parents to feel overly stressed and exhausted as they work to give their kids the best possible care.

Fostering a healthier and more sustainable parenting experience begins with recognizing the warning signals of parental burnout. Parents can proactively address their issues, seek help, and apply methods to prevent burnout by knowing the signs and underlying causes of burnout.

As we set out on this investigation, let's cultivate a shared comprehension that enables parents to put their own health first and establish a more supportive atmosphere for their family.

Signs of Parental Burnout

When you notice any of these signs, know that you are either already burning out or on the verge of burning out. It is preferable to prevent than to cure. We may refer to them as warning signs of parental exhaustion.

- **Persistent fatigue**: Constantly experiencing fatigue, even after taking a break.
- **Emotional numbness**: Losing enthusiasm or delight in rearing children. You lose your temper over your mothering responsibilities excessively.
- **Enhanced irritability**: Finding it easier to become angry with your child.
- **Diminished empathy**: Finding it difficult to relate to your child's emotions.
- **Performance impairment**: Trouble handling day-to-day parent responsibilities.

- **Refusing to fulfill obligations**: Ignoring your parenting responsibilities intentionally.
- **Having frequent guilt**: Constantly feeling guilty about your upbringing.
- **Reduced patience**: Experiencing a rapid loss of tolerance with your spouse or your children.
- **Escapist behaviors**: Using diversions to get out of having to take care of the family.
- **Unusual sleep patterns**: Having trouble getting a good night's sleep.
- **Ignorance**: Often failing to fulfill crucial roles as a parent and you have excuses you consider reasonable.
- **Increased bodily complaints**: Stress-related health problems are becoming more prevalent.
- **Having trouble focusing**: Finding it difficult to concentrate on parenting duties.

- **Relationship tension**: Having trouble establishing a connection with your spouse or pals.
- **Decrease in enjoyment**: You're not as happy spending time with your child as you once were.
- **Increased anxiety**: Experiencing greater trepidation or concern regarding parenthood.
- **Reduced productivity**: Having trouble completing your regular duties.
- Isolation: Withdrawing from social interactions with other parents.
- **A strong sense of obligation**: Experiencing a heavy load from your parental responsibilities.

Recognizing Parental Burnout's Early Warning Signs

Seeing shifts in your feelings, ideas, and actions is one way to see the early warning signs of parental burnout. Keep an eye out for signs of chronic fatigue, overwhelm, heightened irritation, retreating from family events, and a general decline in your wellbeing. It's critical to prioritize self-care and seek support if you observe these symptoms in order to stop burnout from getting worse.

Recognizing the Emotional Cost of Burnout in Parenting

Burnout in parents can be emotionally draining. It is similar to feeling overburdened, tense, and exhausted from all of the ongoing expectations and chores that come with being a parent, such as watching your children and taking care of the house.

Your emotions are negatively impacted by parental burnout, leaving you emotionally spent and mentally spent. It might be difficult for you to handle stress, which could make you feel empty and less able to appreciate the rewarding parts of being a parent. It may affect your disposition, tolerance, and general health.

CHAPTER 2

HOW TO HANDLE PARENTAL BURNOUT

Parents that suffer from parental burnout should be aware that they are burning out. However, it is far more practical for these parents to learn how to deal with it and receive rehabilitation so that they can love being parents rather than endure it.

When parents experience exhaustion and overwhelm from the never-ending obligations of raising children, it's known as parental burnout like I said earlier .It may be brought on by a mix of emotional exhaustion, stress, and a lack of support.

It will be important for us to take into consideration some similar circumstances that could be producing parental fatigue before we go into how to treat it.

Factors That Lead to Parental Burnout

- **Social Expectations**: Parents frequently experience pressure to live up to social norms, such as providing flawless childcare. This might cause burnout as they try to live up to irrational expectations, such as keeping their house immaculate or making sure their kids always succeed academically.
  Parents who pay close attention to what society expects of them and how they are perceived by others may unintentionally begin to work themselves up in an attempt to appear as unblemished as possible in the society evaluation.

SOLUTION:

To deal with this, you should have reasonable expectations and acknowledge that you can't be a perfect parent. When you feel like you're in the deep blue sea when it comes to managing your house, it's also okay to ask for help.

It's also beneficial to express your boundaries. To prevent giving in to social pressure, clearly state your boundaries.

- **Managing job and Family**: Trying to balance the responsibilities of both job and family may be rather difficult. For example, juggling a busy career with attending the kids' extracurricular activities can be difficult for parents, leading to stress and exhaustion.

SOLUTION:

Delegating tasks and setting priorities will help you get past this. Determine what needs to be done and assign assignments when and when you can. You don't have to commit suicide attempting to complete the chores by yourself.

To keep a balance, it's critical that you specify exactly when you work and when you spend time with your family.

- **Isolation and Lack of Support**: Parental burnout may result from feeling alone and without a network of friends or family. For example, if friends or family don't support or understand a parent going through difficult times like insomnia, the parent may burn out more quickly.

SOLUTION:

Try not to let loneliness and a lack of support get to you. Aim to establish a network of support. Make connections with friends, relatives, or other parents to get shared experiences and emotional support.

Seeking help from counselors or therapists is a great idea if you're experiencing symptoms of burnout and loneliness.

MANAGING PARENTAL BURNOUT

The following strategies can also be used to manage parental burnout:

- **Communication**: Discuss duties and feelings honestly with your spouse, and collaborate to create solutions. Misunderstandings that can result in burnout are avoided when there is clear communication.

- **Time management**: Set realistic goals, prioritize your work, and make a timetable that includes breaks. Parents who manage their time well are less likely to burn out because they can better balance job, household responsibilities, and leisure time.

- **Self-Care**: Find little opportunities for exercise, hobbies, or rest. Make self-care a priority. Preserving your physical and emotional health is essential to avoiding burnout.

- **Social Support**: Assemble a network of friends, relatives, or other parents for support. Emotional support and reduction of the stress causing burnout can be obtained by sharing experiences and asking for assistance when required.

- **Flexibility**: Be open to changing your expectations and parenting methods. Reducing the strain that causes burnout can be achieved by accepting that imperfections are common and learning to adjust to changes instead of aiming for an impossibly high standard.

CHAPTER 3

THE IMPACT OF PARENTAL BURNOUT ON PARENT-CHILD RELATIONSHIPS

The bond between parents and children may suffer greatly as a result of parental burnout. Parents who are burned out may suffer from emotional tiredness, decreased efficacy, and heightened detachment. This may result in a decreased ability to attend to their child's needs, which could have an adverse effect on the child's mental health.

Parents may experience a decline in communication and find it difficult to interact positively with their children. In the end, parental burnout can weaken the link between parents and children, which could have long-term effects on the child's growth and the dynamics of the family as a whole.

Parents who experience emotional weariness frequently feel depleted and less able to give their relationships with their children the emotional energy they need. Parents may find it more difficult to successfully manage their child's conduct as a result of their diminished patience due to weariness. As a result, kids can think their parents aren't understanding or supporting them, which would affect their confidence and sense of security.

Another aspect of parental burnout is reduced efficacy, which can result in feelings of inadequacy and self-doubt. Parents could doubt their capacity to assist or attend to their child's demands. Because consistency and dependability in caring are essential for a child's feeling of stability, self-doubt can undermine a parent's confidence when making parenting decisions.

Moreover, emotional detachment may be a result of parental fatigue. Burnout-stricken parents may withdraw emotionally in order to manage their personal pressures. Children who experience this emotional disengagement may feel ignored or unimportant, which can impede the growth of a solid parent-child relationship.

Parental burnout can have long-term effects on parent-child relationships in a number of ways, such as disturbed communication patterns, strained connection, and possible behavioral issues for the child. It emphasizes how crucial it is to take care of parents' wellbeing in order to create a happy, stable home environment.

Envision life as a winding road full of surprises. You make an effort to learn how to manage and adjust to the highs and lows that come with being a parent. Being a parent means that you have to learn to navigate change and adapt to new situations. Undoubtedly, things need to change, and in order to avoid being a burnout parent, you must consciously be prepared to adjust.

Keep lines of communication open. Try not to stomach your challenges with parenting. Talk about it. Open communication can be thought of as having straightforward, honest discussions with someone. In this instance, the issue is how parental fatigue impacts the relationship between parents and children.

You, your partner, and your children can better understand one another's sentiments and cooperate to help one another by talking about these effects.

CHAPTER 4

STRATEGIES FOR MANAGING PARENTAL BURNOUT

Although being a parent is a wonderful and joyful journey, there are many difficulties along the way. Parental burnout is a term used to describe the extreme emotional and physical tiredness that can result from the demands of contemporary parenthood. The stress that parents experience from trying to satisfy their children's demands, take care of the home, and frequently balance work obligations can have a negative impact on their general wellbeing.

Let's examine the phenomena of parental burnout and how it affects people individually as well as in families in this chapter. Having identified the telltale signs and symptoms of parental burnout it is also good to learn some strategies that can be used to manage parental burnout in order to promote a positive parenting experience.

Parents can improve their own mental and emotional health and foster a more loving and supportive environment for their children by learning and using good coping methods.

COPING STRATEGIES FOR PARENTAL BURNOUT

- **Self-Care Techniques**: Scheduling joyful and relaxing activities, such as hobbies or quick getaways, to rejuvenate yourself.
- **Looking for Support Networks**: Making connections with family, friends, or fellow parents in order to exchange experiences and receive emotional support.
- **Realistic Expectations**: To lessen stress and strain, own your limitations and set attainable goals.
- **Mindfulness**: Using methods like deep breathing or meditation to stay present and composed helps to manage burnout faster.

- **Including Mindful Practices**: Including mindful exercises in everyday routines will help you maintain attention and grounding.
- **Developing Resilience**: Creating the emotional fortitude to overcome obstacles and recover from trying circumstances.
- Setting priorities and striking a balance between personal demands and parental responsibilities are two ways to balance responsibilities.
- Task delegation is the practice of dividing up duties among family members or asking for assistance when necessary to reduce workload.
- Managing your time well involves setting priorities and organizing your work so that you have more time for leisure and self-care.
- Working together to divide up parenting duties and reach choices as a couple.
- Collaborating with other parents to establish a stable and nurturing atmosphere for your children.

- Keep a consistent parenting style, be open about issues, expectations, and choices.
- Consult with specialists or make use of materials such as parenting courses, books, and articles.
- Recognize the warning signals of burnout and understand when to seek assistance or back off.
- Seeking treatment or counseling from mental health specialists when necessary.

CHAPTER 5

PREVENTIVE MEASURES FOR PARENTAL BURNOUT

The obligations and difficulties of parenthood can occasionally create a complex pattern in the rich tapestry that results in burnout and tiredness. The possibility of parental burnout becomes a common issue as parents, as caregivers, attempt to fulfill the many needs of their children, navigate the changing dynamics of family life, and handle the daily tasks.

Preventing parental burnout is considerably less expensive than managing it. You can lessen it to a manageable level, even though you can't totally prevent it from happening. Now, let's examine some preventative strategies that can be used to avoid parental burnout.

Strategies to Prevent Parental Burnout

- Make sure you have time and energy set aside for self-care by clearly defining your boundaries.
- Assign parenting responsibilities to your spouse or ask friends and relatives for assistance.
- Make self-care a priority by scheduling time for enjoyable pursuits like reading, working out, or just relaxing.
- Talk to your partner about your wants and emotions to build support and understanding.
- Make sure you get enough sleep to keep your body and mind healthy.
- To increase general resilience, eat a balanced diet and get frequent exercise.
- Plan your days well to strike a balance between work, family, and personal time.
- Take up hobbies or mindfulness exercises to reduce stress and maintain present-moment awareness.

- Choose your obligations wisely to prevent taking on more than you can handle.
- To properly address and manage stressors, seek the advice of a therapist or counselor as needed.
- Acknowledge that being a parent isn't always easy and that it's acceptable when things don't go as planned.
- To raise spirits, recognize and value all of the small victories.
- Promote connections with other parents in order to exchange experiences and offer support to one another.
- Talk about any difficulties or changes that need to be made to your parenting style at regular check-ins with your spouse.
- Keep up personal pursuits that you find fulfilling and enjoyable away from parenting.
- Give yourself the tools you need to handle your stress, like progressive muscle relaxation or deep breathing.

- Create a loving and supportive environment for your children by emphasizing positive reinforcement.
- Keep up with parenting techniques and kid growth to face obstacles with more assurance.
- Schedule regular family activities to build stronger bonds and lasting memories. Establish Quality Family Time.
- Develop an attitude of thankfulness by recognizing and appreciating the good things in your family's existence.

Open Discussions on Parental Burnout by Some Women.

Let's examine the topic these women are discussing and how they were able to find answers.

Danielle: *You know, I've simply been feeling so overwhelmed by parenting these days. It seems as though the demands never stop.*

Catherine: *You are heard. It wears me out. I question whether I'm doing anything correctly at times.*

Josephine: *It's the same here, really. It seems as though we have to accomplish everything and leave no room for ourselves.*

Danielle: *I've tried a lot of coping mechanisms, but nothing seems to stick.*

Catherine: Perhaps we should figure out how to help each other more effectively. Discuss what functions well and poorly.

Josephine: I concur. It's time to put our health first. How about if we set modest, manageable objectives for ourselves?

Danielle: In what way?

Catherine: Perhaps setting out a certain period of time every week for self-care. Take a solitary stroll, indulge in a book, or simply take a peaceful bath.

Josephine: And how about we talk about our challenges more honestly? We don't have to act as though nothing is wrong.

Danielle: That seems very freeing. We all need that room, I suppose, to be vulnerable.

Catherine: Certainly. Don't be afraid to seek assistance. It could come from our friends, *partners, or even from periodically hiring a babysitter.*

Josephine: What if we established a network of support and kept each other updated on a regular basis? Talk about our victories and setbacks.

Danielle: I adore that concept. Knowing we're not the only ones experiencing this could be really beneficial.

[After making these adjustments for a few weeks]

Catherine: I feel so much better than I can believe. It has changed everything for me to take that time for myself.

Josephine: I agree completely. Furthermore, sharing my troubles with others relieved me of a burden. I had no idea that we were all experiencing comparable experiences.

Danielle: When we help one another, amazing things happen. I now feel more capable and energized.

Catherine: We have developed a home treatment for burnout among parents.

Josephine: And we completed it in unison. When we rely on one another, we get stronger.

Always Remember This

You don't have to be flawless. Parenting has hurdles, therefore it's critical to give self-care first priority. Create a network of support, be honest with your partner, and don't be afraid to ask for assistance when you need it. In the end, taking care of your health and well-being will benefit you and your kids.

IMPORTANT LESSONS

The cultivation of awareness through techniques such as meditation can lower stress levels, improve concentration, and improve general well being. This is why mindfulness matters.

- **Balanced Lifestyle**: To promote both physical and mental health, make sleep, frequent exercise, and healthy food your top priorities. Establishing and preserving significant connections with others is essential as it promotes a feeling of acceptance and has a favorable effect on psychological health.

- **Continuous Learning**: Embrace a growth mindset, pursue lifelong learning, and set achievable goals to foster personal and professional development.

- **Practice Gratitude**: Consistently expressing thanks for life's blessings can boost happiness and improve one's perspective.

- **Quality Rest**: Prioritize quality sleep to enhance cognitive function, mood regulation, and overall resilience.

- **Digital Detox**: Moderate your use of technology to enhance your wellbeing. Periodic digital detoxes can lower stress and improve mental health.

- **Self-compassion**: Remember that everyone has difficulties and failures, and treat yourself with compassion and understanding.

Recall that applying these ideas to your everyday life promotes long-term health and a more contented life.

CONCLUSION

To sum up, "Parental Burnout: How to Cope with the Stress and Exhaustion of Parenting" is an understanding manual and a ray of hope for parents negotiating the difficult terrain of parenting kids in the competitive world of today.

In addition to shedding light on the widespread problem of parental burnout, the book provides helpful advice and insightful solutions to assist parents in regaining their wellbeing and rediscovering the joy of parenting. It's clear from reading this book's pages that parental burnout is a complex issue that calls for an all-encompassing solution.

The book also promotes a culture that recognizes and supports parents' well-being, which calls for a change in how society views parenting. The author gives parents the tools to accept imperfection, ask for help when necessary, and put their own mental and emotional well-being first by demolishing the myth of the ideal parent and advocating for a more pragmatic and sympathetic viewpoint.

"Parental Burnout" is essentially a lifesaver for parents who are drowning in their to-do list. It's more than just a book. It conveys a message of resiliency, optimism, and the realization that asking for assistance is acceptable.

When parents close the book on their parenting journey, they do so with a newfound sense of purpose and a toolkit of doable tactics to help them face the obstacles head-on. The transformational power of self-awareness, self-compassion, and the steadfast love that drives the amazing adventure of parenthood is demonstrated in this book.

Dear reader,

I appreciate you reading "Parental Burnout" so much. Your attempt to read this book demonstrates your unwavering dedication to both your own and your family's well-being. I really thank you for taking the time to read this.

Please assist me in passing along this book's material to others who might find it useful.

My email address is:
parentingchildrenandfamily@yahoo.com.

Printed in Dunstable, United Kingdom